ONLY IN
TEXAS

ONLY IN
TEXAS

*What's Bigger,
Better, and Larger than Life
in the Lone Star State*

CARRIE SHOOK
and
ROBERT L. SHOOK

A Perigee Book

Perigee Books
are published by
The Putnam Publishing Group
200 Madison Avenue
New York, NY 10016

Photographs of Sea World © 1989 by Sea World, Inc.
Used by permission.

Library of Congress Cataloging-in-Publication Data

Shook, Carrie.
    Only in Texas: what's bigger, better, and larger than life in the
Lone Star State / by Carrie Shook and Robert L. Shook.
        p.   cm.
    1. Texas—Miscellanea.   2. Texas—Description and travel—
1981–   —Guide-books.
I. Shook Robert L., date.   II. Title.
ISBN 0-399-51557-7
F386.5.S55   1989   89-16121 CIP
976.4—dc20

Printed in the United States of America

1   2   3   4   5   6   7   8   9   10

Contents

Acknowledgments   9

Map   10

Texas Jokes   11

Introduction   13

The Texas State Capitol   15

Festivals and Barbecues, Texas Style   17

The Black-eyed Pea Jamboree   18

The Uncle Fletch Davis Home
of the Hamburger Cook-off   21

The Fire Ant Festival   22

The Poteet Strawberry Festival   23

The Texas Citrus Fiesta   24

The Watermelon Thump   25

The Wurstfest   26

Fiesta del Concho / Fort Concho   28

Bar B Ques . . . Only in Texas!   31

The Chilympiad   33

The State Fair of Texas   36

The Tallest Cowboy in the World   37

Sea World of Texas · 39

The World's Only Flying Whale   41

Texas: A Rustic Alternative to Broadway   42

Whooping It Up in Texas   45

The Lyndon B. Johnson Space Center   47

The Astrodome: Eighth Wonder of the World   50

The Dallas/Fort Worth Airport   52

Aquarena Springs   54

The Ghost Squadron   55

The River Walk   57

The First Columbus   59

Texas Nightlife   64

Gilley's   65

The Swingingest Laundromat in the World   67

Miss Hattie's   68

Is That a Chicken in Your Pocket,
or Are You Just Glad to See Me?   71

Texas Ladies Aside   72

The Rodeo   73

The Mesquite Championship Rodeo   75

The San Angelo Stock Show and Rodeo   77

The XIT Ranch   79

The King Ranch   81

The Cadillac Ranch   84

The Big Texan Steak Ranch   86

The Governor's Mansion   88

Southfork Ranch   90

The Beer Can House   92

A Princely Home . . . at a Prince's Ransom   93

Texas Money   94
Striking It Rich at Spindletop   95
The World's Richest Acre   98
Highways Paved with Gold   100
The Neiman Marcus Christmas Book   101
A Millionaire's Million Air   104
The Texans!   105
Stephen F. Austin   106
Sam Houston   108
The Alamo—A Shrine to Texas Liberty   110
The Texas Rangers   112
The Real Ima Hogg   114
The Palace on Wheels   116
Think Pink   118
Santa Claus: The Bank Robber   120
The Rangerettes of Kilgore   122
A Deliberate Disaster   123
The Traveling Hotel   126
Funeral for a Baby-blue Ferrari   127

Acknowledgments

We would like to thank the following people for their tremendous contributions: Elisabeth Adair-Jaffe, Mary Kay Ash, Brett Battles, Paul Bendel, Bud Brooks, Larry Burruss, Lainey Cohen, Liz Conover, Patty Fletcher, Anil Gangolli, Evelyn Hill, Mary Liff, Stanley Marsh 3, Joyce Martin, Lisa McLemore, Mary Milkovisch, Anne Myers, Joe Myers, Jason Plummer, Buddy Rau, Kara Read, Mary Richter, Becky Smith, Annie Bell Taylor, and David Tornes for his illustrations.

We would also like to thank the chambers of commerce throughout the state that gave us their valuable assistance; and Ann Lee and Associates, Aransas National Wildlife Refuge, Bayou Bend, Beaumont Chamber of Commerce, Columbus Tourist Development Committee, Dallas Convention & Visitors Bureau, Dallas/Fort Worth International Airport, Fairmount Hotel, Governor's Mansion, Houston Astro Baseball Club, Jessie Allen Wise Garden Club, Kilgore Chamber of Commerce, King Ranch, Mary Kay Cosmetics, Inc., Mesquite Championship Rodeo, Million Air, NASA, Neiman Marcus, Palo Duro Canyon State Park, San Angelo Convention and Visitors Bureau, San Angelo Stock Show and Rodeo, Sea World of Texas, Southfork Ranch, Southwest Airlines, State Fair of Texas, State Department of Highways and Public Transportation, Texas Collection of Baylor University, and the cast and crew of the musical *Texas*.

Special Acknowledgment

We would like to thank our editors, Lindley Boegehold and Tina Isaac, for their creative force and dedicated effort.

Texas Jokes

Texans are known for their sense of humor, and they particularly like telling jokes about their enormous state. Here are a few favorites:

TEXAN: Where you from, stranger?

STRANGER: I'm from Ohio.

TEXAN: Ohio? Mmm, I don't think I've ever been to that part of Texas.

Three Texans—two tall macho ones, and a small, frail one—are drinking at a bar. The two tall Texans are bragging about their ranches.

FIRST TALL TEXAN: Yep, my ranch goes thirty miles north and twenty-five miles to the south. It goes for twenty miles west and another twenty-eight miles east.

SECOND TALL TEXAN: What do you call your ranch?

FIRST TALL TEXAN: (boastfully) I call it the BRX Ranch.

SECOND TALL TEXAN: That's quite a spread. But not as big as mine. My ranch goes thirty-five miles north and forty miles to the south. It goes for fifty miles west and more than sixty miles east.

FIRST TALL TEXAN: Man, *that* is big. What do you call your place?

SECOND TALL TEXAN: (proudly) I call it the TXT Ranch.

They turn to the small, frail man next to them.

FIRST TEXAN: How big is your ranch, little man?

SMALL TEXAN: Oh, about one square mile.

With that they both howl.

FIRST TEXAN: That's a mighty small spread you got there, little man. And may I ask what you call it?

SMALL TEXAN: Downtown Dallas.

FIRST TEXAN: It takes me all day to ride my pickup across my ranch.

SECOND TEXAN: Yep, I once had a pickup like yours.

TEXAN: I would like to withdraw sixty million dollars from my petty-cash account.

BANKER: What on earth for?

TEXAN: I've decided to air-condition Texas.

Q. What's the most popular type of furniture in Texas?
A. "Oily" American.

Introduction

Texas! The only state in the union bigger than life itself. Texas has a culture all its own, as well as a distinct identity famous from Great Britain to Zimbabwe.

Only in Texas includes descriptions of the colorful and outrageous places, people, and events that could be found only in Texas. They range from grand to gaudy, from magnificent to bizarre. You will find what makes this state unique.

Texas was once an independent country, as well as a territory governed by various foreign governments. Somehow it has never gotten rid of the notion of being different. It is a huge state, about the size of France, as large as all of New England, New York, Pennsylvania, Ohio, and Illinois combined. It has a diverse political background; six different flags have flown over Texas, and there have been eight different governments:

Spain	1519–1685
France	1685–1690
Spain	1690–1821
Mexico	1821–1836
Republic of Texas	1836–1845
United States	1845–1861
Confederate States	1861–1865
United States	1865–present

In 1845, Texas was accepted into the Union. A condition that appears in the resolution approving its statehood is the option to subdivide into as many as four more states (a total of five). Texas does not have the right to secede any more than any other state.

Early Texas history laid the groundwork for the state's mythological stature. The Battle of the Alamo is one of the most famous in the history of North America: the siege at the Alamo lasted almost two weeks, ending on March 6, 1836, with only 187 Texans holding their own against a Mexican army of about 4,000 soldiers. Famous Texans killed in the battle were Davy Crockett, Jim Bowie, and William B. Travis. The subsequent massacre of Texans who surrendered at Goliad on March 27 led to the famous battle cry of Texas independence: "Remember the Alamo!" was instilled into the mind of every Texan.

Until Alaska entered the Union, Texas was by far the largest state. It covers 267,339 square miles, seven percent of the entire land mass of the United States, and is larger than any country in Western Europe. At its widest, Texas measures 801 miles from point to point. The state has over 6,300 square miles of inland lakes and streams. Over 70,000 miles of highway are strung throughout Texas, more than in all the Soviet Union. A rich, diverse history permeates the 10,000 landmarks and 35,000 archaeological sites throughout the state.

Dimensions like these make it fitting that everything in Texas comes in extralarge sizes. The "Texas-sized" seventy-two-ounce steak, for example, is a Texas-proud portion. Everything in Texas seems *big*, from the "big spread" and "big oil" to Big Tex.

Around the world, Texas is associated with romance, adventure, valor, and the Old West, which is still alive and kicking. You can still find "Old Texas" cattle and horse ranches and wealthy, wheeler-dealer "J.R." oilmen. Yet so much lies beyond these stereotypes: this remarkable state has a culture all its own, and Texans hold on proudly to the notion of being different.

14

The Texas State Capitol

What would be expected of Texas when it comes to building a state capitol? It would have to be the largest, most impressive state capitol you could imagine. Completed in May 1888, the Texas State Capitol with its 308-foot spire is the tallest in the country—taller even than our nation's capitol. It is 566 feet wide and boasts 392 rooms. All of the materials used in it are native to Texas, from the majestic pink granite of the walls and the cast iron of the columns to the brass and marble of decorative details.

At the time the capitol was built, Texas was larger than it is now, with boundaries extending as far northwest as Wyoming. A wave of progress had begun and constructing a building to house the young government was a top priority. The location of a state capital was a major issue in the 1850, 1870, and 1872 Texas elections. Austin was declared the capital, its 64,000 votes beating 35,000 for Houston and 13,000 for Waco.

For a price of 3-million-plus acres of Texas land sprawled across ten Panhandle counties, two contractors from Chicago agreed to build the capitol in Austin. Charles B. and John V. Farwell constructed the $3.2 million building and turned the more than 3 million acres into the famous XIT Ranch.

The Texas State Capitol in Austin.
(Courtesy Texas Senate Media Services)

Festivals and Barbecues, Texas Style

Texans celebrate just about anything you could imagine with a festival. They honor mosquitoes, rattlesnakes, sausages, clams, strawberries, grapefruits, watermelons, spinach, and yams. They have a reputation for accepting anything as a reason for a good time. Their barbecues are world-famous, and they like to do things up Texas style.

17

The Black-eyed Pea Jamboree

Athens, Texas, the black-eyed pea capital of the world, is the location for the Black-eyed Pea Jamboree, a celebration of the vegetable that has brought substantial income to the community. Over 35,000 visitors attend the annual festival, held the third weekend in July. The jamboree features a well-rounded calendar of events: adults' and children's cook-offs for the best original black-eyed pea recipes, pea-popping-and-shelling competitions, and of course a contest for Miss Black-eyed Pea and Little Miss Black-eyed Pea. There are also over 200 arts-and-crafts booths; five-kilometer, ten-kilometer and one-mile fun runs; and a Black-eyed Pea Bike Tour. Other highlights include booths offering homemade black-eyed-pea–flavored ice cream, gospel music, a children's pet show, and the Pea-Pickers' Square Dance.

The 1988 grand champion, Bertha Anne Hatton of Murchison, won the cook-off with the following old-fashioned recipe:

Granny's Pea Potpie

   3 cups cooked black-eyed peas, chopped (use dry, not canned, peas)
   1 lb. fresh mushrooms, chopped
   1 cup chopped onions
   3 tbsp. melted butter

1/4 tsp. thyme

1/2 tsp. salt

1/8 tsp. pepper

1/2 tsp. garlic salt

2 tbsp. flour

1/4 cup sour cream

1 lb. sausage, cooked and crumbled

3/4 cup cheddar cheese

2 tbsp. pimientos, chopped

2 ready-to-bake pie shells

Cook dry peas in boiling water until soft; drain water and then chop peas. Sauté mushrooms and onions in butter until tender. Add thyme, salt, pepper, garlic salt, and flour; mix well. Stir in sour cream and sausage. Cook over low heat until mixture thickens. Stir in peas, cheese, and pimientos and set mixture aside. Place first pie shell in 9-inch pie plate and fill with pea mixture. Place second pie shell on top of mixture and seal. Cut slits in top shell and cook at 400 degrees for 12–15 minutes or until golden brown. Makes 1 potpie.

The second-place winner in 1988 was Nell Swinney of Rowlett. Her recipe represents black-eyed pea cooking in the eighties:

Black-eyed Pea-ta Pockets

1/2 lb. bacon, fried, cooled, and crumbled (save drippings)

1/2 small head lettuce, shredded

2 medium tomatoes, peeled and chopped (remove seeds)

1/2 medium onion, chopped

1/2 cup shredded cheddar cheese

2 avocados, chopped, and sprinkled with 2 tbsp. lemon juice

2 cups black-eyed peas, cooked and drained

19

salt and pepper, to taste
mayonnaise, to taste
6 pita pockets (12 halves)

Mix all ingredients. Pour 2 tbsp. bacon drippings over mixture, and moisten with mayonnaise. Cut pita rounds in half and fill. Serves 6.

You could make an entire meal out of black-eyed peas, starting with past cook-off winners such as black-eyed pea martinis and black-eyed pea ice cream for dessert. Wear some black-eyed pea cologne or perfume for the occasion!

The Uncle Fletch Davis
Home of the Hamburger
Cook-off

Few know that Athens, Texas, is also the birthplace of the hamburger. First created in the 1880s by Fletcher Davis (known to Athenians as "Uncle Fletch"), Uncle Fletch's specialty consisted of a ground-meat patty served between two slices of homemade bread, with hot mustard, a thick slice of Bermuda onion, and a cucumber pickle on the side. The sandwich was introduced by Uncle Fletch at the 1904 World's Fair in St. Louis. He sold his sandwiches from a booth on the midway and introduced the newest sandwich innovation to people from all over the world.

Since 1984, Athens has held a yearly Uncle Fletch Home of the Hamburger Cook-off on the fourth Saturday of each September. There are all kinds of entertainment: a carnival, a street dance—the Burger Ball—arts and crafts, and even a "bun run," in which contestants put hamburger buns between their knees and race around a course! But the highlight of the day is the cook-off, where contestants can use any type of recipe they want. Humongous hamburgers have been made out of all types of meat mixed together—beef, deer, pork, and snake. Homemade buns are always a hit. The Uncle Fletch Home of the Hamburger Cook-off is growing bigger each year and will continue for generations. Athenians insist: "We are the Home of the Hamburger!"

The Fire Ant Festival

Every October in Marshall, natives celebrate the fire ant at a festival that attracts over 40,000 visitors. Perhaps the wackiest festival in all of Texas, it features outrageous activities that non-Texans have a hard time believing. The fire ant, known for its color and its sting, is usually considered a pest. But here the Fire Ant Roundup requires contestants to collect as many fire ants as they can in a gallon-sized milk container over a four-hour period.

The fire ant calling contest is always a thrill, as nobody *really* knows what noise, if any, a fire ant makes. Contestants must imitate three calls: a mating call, an alarm call, and a feeding call. A pet show awards first place to the contestant most resembling a fire ant. The high point of the weekend is the chili cook-off: recipes must have at least one fire ant somewhere in the chili—this is only for those who like their chili served extra hot! (The weekend is sponsored by the American Cyanamid Company, which manufactures Amdro, an insecticide used to kill fire ants.)

The Poteet Strawberry Festival

The Poteet Strawberry Festival, one of the oldest and largest festivals in Texas, is held in the strawberry capital of Texas and attracts up to 100,000 strawberry fans. Once a year, on a weekend in April, you can sample a smorgasbord of delicacies, from strawberry shortcakes, cheesecakes, and parfaits to strawberry wines and cheeses. Only in Poteet can you see the world's largest statue of a strawberry (six feet tall weighing 1,600 pounds).

The Texas Citrus Fiesta

For over fifty years the Texas Citrus Fiesta has taken place in Mission, "Home of the Grapefruit." The annual event, held the last two weeks in January, offers the unique Product Costume Style Show, the Parade of Oranges with covered floats, and the crowning of the Royal Citrus Family, King Citrus and Queen Citrianna presiding.

The haute couture of the Product Costume Style Show, with models decked out in leaves, flowers, fruits, vegetables, and citrus peel, dates back to the first fiesta in 1932. This brand of costume design is believed to be the only new folk art introduced in Texas in this century. A typical costume is described thus: "A formula of poinsettia bracts, hibiscus, bougainvillea, purple onions, and beets adorn the skirt, bodice, and sleeve caps of our model's very formal gown. Ground corn covers the chenille trim of her elbow-length sleeves, and the white lace accents on her sleeve caps are made of flaked onion skins and squash seeds. Grapefruit rag and white onion skin are arranged into a festive floral headpiece." Fiesta gowns often take over 100 hours to create, yet cost as little as $16. Fiesta costumes have been featured in magazines and shows around the world.

The Parade of Oranges, also one of a kind, features floats containing at least fifty percent natural products grown in the valley. The parade winds through downtown Mission streets, lined with over 100,000 spectators. The only thing models have to worry about is being eaten alive by fruit-loving insects!

The Watermelon Thump

The yearly June Watermelon Thump celebrates Luling's most important resource—the watermelon. The Thump, which attracts over 30,000 visitors, crowns a Watermelon Thump queen and has food booths with watermelon specialties, a parade, and of course a PRCA rodeo (sanctioned by the Professional Rodeo Cowboys Association). There is also a car rally, melon-eating contests, and an auction of the top melons.

Other highlights include the seed-spitting contest and the watermelon championship. The *Guinness Book of World Records* recognizes the longest seed-spit in history as 65 feet, 4 inches, by John Wilkinson at the 1980 festival. Wilkinson, coincidentally, repeated the feat in 1981. The seed-spitting contest attracts international attention and has been featured by *U.S. News & World Report* and *Today*.

Traditionally, the popular Black Diamond Watermelon is the only acceptable variety for championship honors. It is emerald green (and not striped) and oval, and grows to enormous sizes. Since the first festival in 1954, the largest Black Diamond champion was an 80-pounder, in 1962. The champion melon is presented to a celebrity; past honorees have been Johnny Carson, Art Linkletter, and Ronald Reagan.

The Luling Watermelon Thump is on the move. Enjoy the biggest, juiciest watermelons you've ever seen, but watch out for fast-flying seeds!

The Wurstfest

This annual sausage festival takes place in New Braunfels, the sausage capital of the United States. Over 100 years ago, a number of German immigrants settled in New Braunfels, bringing with them recipes from the old country which have been handed down from generation to generation.

The mouth-watering flavors of the original sausage recipes have not changed, and at the Wurstfest you will find patrons dressed in combinations of Old World dirndls and lederhosen, as well as jeans and cowboy boots. Rated among the world's top attractions, the November festival lures over 150,000 visitors. Forty-two tons of sausage are consumed, entertainment is provided by local German singing clubs, and proud dachshund owners may enter their pets in the Sausage Hound Dog Show. Visitors can also tour the world's largest beer bottle collection, donated to the Wurstfest Association by Jerome Newotny.

Only in Texas can you spend a day in Germany without crossing the ocean!

Entertainment, German style, at the Wurstfest.
(Courtesy Wurstfest Association of New Braunfels)

Fiesta del Concho/Fort Concho

The Fiesta del Concho, held each June in San Angelo, is a citywide celebration of agriculture in the Concho Valley, centering around a large western dance, sheepshearing, a quilt show, and sheepdog trials. Fort Concho, a national historic landmark, commemorates local late-nineteenth-century frontier life.

The San Angelo area is the largest wool and mohair producer in the United States, so it is a natural location for the Texas State Sheep Shearing Contest. Shearers competing for the state title are judged and scored on shearing time, condition of fleece, absence of cuts in fleece, manner of handling sheep, and the beauty of the shorn sheep's new 'do. The winner represents Texas in the national championships, held each January in Denver.

Sheepdog trials are another favorite attraction. Dog and handler are judged on skills at herding sheep. Handlers direct the dogs with voice commands, hand signals, and whistles to move, stop, or "cut out" sheep, through a course that includes obstacles, open ground, and chutes.

Founded in 1867, Fort Concho was the stronghold in a line of forts built to protect settlers from Indian attack at the confluence of two branches of the Concho River. The Fort Concho Museum exhibits relics from Indian wars and frontier days. A popular "living" exhibit at the museum is a group of volunteers who portray members of

Texas State Sheep Shearing Contest at the Fiesta del Concho in San Angelo. (Photo by Joe Abell)

historic military groups. The Fort Concho Memorial Infantry, Cavalry, and the famous Buffalo Soldiers (black enlisted men of the frontier) demonstrate their skills and drills, and fire authentic Springfield rifles and carbines. The Enlisted Men's Barracks V houses original beds and equipment used when the fort was an active post. Also on the grounds are authentically restored mess hall, chapel, and schoolhouse. Museum hours are from 10:00 A.M. to 5:00 P.M. Monday through Saturday and 1:00 to

A contestant shears a sheep. (Photo by Joe Abell)

5:00 P.M. on Sunday. Call (915) 657-4441 for more information.

While you are in San Angelo, you must eat at famous Zentner's Daughter steakhouse, founded by octogenarian John Zentner, whose career in the steak business started when he prepared meals for cavalry officers at Camp Stanley (north of San Antonio) in 1918. Hundreds of devoted West Texas customers rave about it and say that whenever they are within 100 miles of the restaurant, they drop in for one of Zentner's thick, juicy steaks.

Bar B Ques . . . Only in Texas!

Barbecues are taken seriously in Texas.

60 Minutes' Harry Reasoner once said, "No one appreciates a piece of burnt prime beef quite like a Texan." Walter Jetton, Lyndon Johnson's personal barbecuer, was dubbed King of the Barbecue and barbecued for every important dignitary who visited the LBJ Ranch.

Home-style barbecuing has grown furiously—there are now hundreds of commercial establishments offering this type of cooking in central Texas alone. Barbecued brisket, ribs, chicken, sausage, steaks, and hamburgers are the most popular, but sheep, goat, lizard, and rattlesnake meat can also be grilled delicacies.

Barbecue cook-offs are a hard-core Texan tradition. Since 1947, the world's largest free barbecue is at the current XIT Ranch—part of what was once the largest range in the world under fence—in honor of the cowboys who first worked there. In recent years, crowds at the XIT Rodeo and Reunion have numbered over 20,000; cornbread, chili, and steaks with all the trimmings are served, and the reunion hosts the world's largest nonprofessional rodeo.

Chili, a Texas invention, is usually made with beef but can also contain venison, rabbit, or other game. The original San Antonio treat did not contain tomatoes but was a simple stew of meat and peppers. Official spicy Texas chili, known as chili con carne (chili with meat), tastes like liquid fire. Chili

31

was a popular dish in the White House during LBJ's administration, and he had standing orders that it be on hand on *Air Force One* at all times.

The presidential chili was prepared by Johnson's cook, Zephyr Wright. It is named after the river that runs in front of the LBJ Ranch in Stonewall. Johnson used to eat it with saltines and a glass of milk.

Pedernales River Chili

4 lbs. beef, coarsely ground

1 large onion, finely chopped

2 cloves garlic, finely chopped

1 tsp. ground oregano

1 tsp. cumin seed

6 tsp. chili powder (add more if desired)

2 16-ounce cans tomatoes

2 cups hot water

salt, to taste

In a heavy stewpot, brown the meat in its own fat until it loses its pink color. Add onion and garlic and cook until onion is translucent. Add remaining ingredients, bring to boil, lower heat and simmer for an hour, covered. Skim off the grease. Add salt to taste. Serves 8.

The Chilympiad

The annual Republic of Texas Men's State Championship Chili Cook-off in San Marcos, held the third weekend of September, is the largest cook-off in Texas. Over 500 cooks compete, and a celebrity panel of 200 judges taste away in four different stages of judging (preliminary, quarter-finals, semifinals, and finals). Celebrity judges (including stars from *Hee Haw*) narrow the field down to twenty-five chili dishes that compete on the final table.

The 1988 Chilympiad winner was Leslie Doss of Austin, who offers his recipe with a bit of advice: "A good recipe does not necessarily make a good chili. It's the tender care the cook takes during preparation. The last thirty-five to forty minutes of cooking are the most important."

3 lbs. top choice beef shoulder (or rattlesnake in season), cubed

2 tbsp. vegetable oil

1 cup chopped onions

1 clove garlic, chopped

1 6-oz. can tomato paste

2 cups water or broth

1 jalapeño pepper, chopped

1 tbsp. chili powder

1 tbsp. red pepper

1 tbsp. white pepper

$^1\!/_2$ tsp. salt

$^3\!/_4$ tsp. oregano

$^2\!/_3$ tsp. cumin

Brown meat in oil, add remaining ingredients, and cook covered for 3 hours or until meat is tender. Let simmer for 1 hour. Serves about 15 (8-ounce portions).

Chili cooks are very private about disclosing secret recipes. The 1988 world champion was Lynn Hejtmancik of Spicewood, Texas. He has generously offered us his winning recipe:

2 tbsp. olive oil

3 lbs. small-cube chuck

2 tbsp. paprika

4 tbsp. jalapeño juice

1 tbsp. plus 5 tsp. garlic powder

1 tbsp. plus 2 tsp. onion powder

$^1\!/_2$ tsp. finely ground black pepper

$^1\!/_4$ tsp. oregano

1 13$^3\!/_4$-ounce can beef broth (preferably Swanson's)

2 beef bouillon cubes

1 8-oz. can tomato sauce (preferably Contadina)

2 tbsp. cumin powder

6 tbsp. straight chili powder (no salt)

2 tsp. hot chili powder

1 tsp. MSG (optional)

pinch brown sugar

Heat oil in a cooking pot. Brown meat and remove unwanted parts. Add paprika, 2 tbsp. jalapeño juice, 1 tbsp. each garlic and onion powder, $^1\!/_4$ tsp. pepper, oregano, broth, and bouillon

34

cubes. Add enough water to cover meat (with 1 inch over meat). Cook covered over medium heat, stirring every 10 minutes until meat is tender. This may take several hours. Skim off unwanted grease, add remaining ingredients, and bring to a boil. Taste and fine-tune if necessary with garlic, cumin, cayenne pepper, hot chili powder, white pepper, or salt. If the chili is too thick you can thin it with beef broth or water; if it is too thin, add arrowroot. Serves about 15 (8-ounce portions).

Secret ingredients in chili recipes range from Chinese five spices to anything that would impart a distinctive flavor. Ingredients are basically the same from chef to chef but may vary in amount, and cooking times tend to differ. In contests, judges will taste only one or two teaspoons of each dish. So be aware that championship-winning recipes are highly concentrated for competition. These recipes may need to be moderated with arrowroot or potato flakes. Flour is not recommended.

The State Fair of Texas

Fairs did not originate in the U.S., but they have become a distinctly American phenomenon. Across the country, over 3,000 annual fairs draw crowds in excess of 150 million, more than double the yearly attendance at professional football and baseball games and Broadway shows combined.

The State Fair of Texas, which has been held since 1887, is the largest and to many the grandest state fair in the country. For eighteen days each October, Dallas hosts the exposition, which features sporting and theatrical events, parades, a rodeo, livestock shows, agricultural exhibitions, and other competitive events. Over 3 million visitors stop in—the record single-day attendance for any state fair was 355,231, at the 1971 Texas State Fair.

The biggest state fair event is *the* big game—Texas versus Oklahoma at the Cotton Bowl. Over 72,000 avid football fans flood the arena for the yearly contest; in 1984 the game sold out for the thirty-eighth consecutive year.

Another immensely popular event is the State Fair Rodeo, where more than 500 of the nation's top cowboys gather to compete for prize money. The rodeo, ranked tops by the Professional Rodeo Cowboys Association, is a three-day event with six separate competitions: saddle bronc riding, bull riding, steer wrestling, bareback bronc riding, calf roping, and girls' barrel racing.

The Tallest Cowboy in the World

The most famous symbol of the Texas State Fair is Big Tex, a fifty-two-foot-tall statue wired for sound who welcomes visitors with hearty Texas warmth: "Howdy, folks, this is Big Tex."

Originally a Santa Claus in the town of Kerens, Tex was sold to fair officials in 1951 for $750 and transformed into a cowboy by a local artist. Now with a wardrobe from the H. D. Lee Company, he proudly wears the largest pair of jeans in the world—size 276 Lee jeans, with a twenty-three-foot waist size. His shirt is red, trimmed in blue and white (the three colors of the Lone Star flag). A seventy-five-gallon cowboy hat tops Tex's costume, and his enormous feet are shod in size 70 tan boots, over seven and a half feet high.

Each year, a week before the fair, Big Tex is assembled and lowered into his boots with a hydraulic crane. It takes a whopping 300 pounds of equipment for Big Tex to greet all who pass by during the fair.

Big Tex greets visitors at the State Fair.
(Courtesy State Fair of Texas)

Sea World of Texas

Sea World of Texas is the largest marine life showplace in the world. Located on 250 scenic acres eighteen miles northwest of San Antonio, it has played host to thousands eager to witness spectacular performances of killer whales, dolphins, sea lions, and penguins.

The star of the show is 5,000-pound Shamu, accompanied by Namu and Kandu, all three expertly trained professional-entertainer killer whales who can jump as high as twenty feet out of the water. The whales, who arrived aboard a 747 jumbo jet, now live in a 7-million-gallon tank, the largest marine mammal facility in the world. The facility accommodates 4,500 spectators and is used for entertainment as well as research and training and as a breeding ground.

Another fascinating Sea World exhibit is the coral reef environment, featuring the largest collection of Indo-Pacific fish in the world. A 300,000-gallon tank is home to seven types of sharks and seventy other kinds of fish. Large sharks and sawfish live in a 450,000-gallon shark aquarium. Sea World has six species of penguins, who live and play in a snowy Antarctic environment. Those who wish can pet and feed dolphins, sea lions, and seals at the Marine Mammal Pool.

Sea World opens year-round at 10:00 A.M.; closing times

vary, with extended hours during the summer and on holidays. Call (512) 523-3611 for a recording of up-to-date information on hours of operation.

World-famous killer whale Shamu at Sea World of Texas.
(Courtesy Sea World, Inc.)

The World's Only Flying Whale

Only one flying killer whale in the world has ever existed outside water: *Shamu One,* a Southwest Airlines Boeing 737-300 airplane distinctively marked to match the real Shamu of Sea World. Shamu represents a strong friendship between Southwest Airlines and Sea World of Texas. The airline offers special travel packages, allowing patrons to purchase airline tickets, accommodations, and passes to Sea World at substantial savings. Call (800) 531-5601 for reservations. Passengers on Southwest flights can use their ticket receipts for a fifteen-percent discount on the regular ticket price to Sea World, if redeemed within ninety days of their flight.

Southwest Airlines' Flying Shamu. (Courtesy Southwest Airlines)

Texas:
A Rustic Alternative to Broadway

The bottom of Palo Duro Canyon State Park in the Texas Panhandle is the stage for the only show in the world presented 600 feet below ground level. *Texas,* by prize-winning Paul Green, is one of the highest-rated attractions in the state. Eighty performers re-create the settling of the Texas Panhandle in the 1880s in this musical drama with beautiful costumes and incredible special effects, which produce realistic thunder and lightning—and even a prairie fire.

An Old West–style barbecue before each performance provides a warm, social way to start the evening. After the barbecue, patrons enter the outdoor amphitheater to see the play. Since performances began in 1966, *Texas* has been seen by over 2 million people.

In outdoor theater, as in real life, one must always prepare for the unexpected. Wacky circumstances during the history of the musical add an extra touch to its already rich history: A horse in the cast once took a bite out of a car in the parking lot. A runaway train used as a prop once chugged right over a performer's banjo. A lead dancer once danced right off the stage. And in one performance, the actor playing Indian chief Quanah Parker meant to strike his spear on the ground for emphasis, but instead drove it clear through his foot!

Performances are held nightly except Sunday from late June through late August. The musical begins at 8:30 P.M. Reservations are advisable. For further information on *Texas,* call (806) 655-2181.

Sit beneath the towering cliffs of Palo Duro Canyon as you watch Texas. (Courtesy cast and crew of *Texas*)

Chief Quanah Parker of the musical Texas.

(Photos courtesy
cast and crew of *Texas*)

An Indian brave leaps through the air in Texas.

Whooping It Up in Texas

The "whoopers" of Texas are the only indigenous wild population of whooping cranes in the world. They live in the Aransas National Wildlife Refuge in Austwell. An experimental flock of whooping cranes that began with just under twenty birds now numbers more than 150 (current world population for this endangered species is around 195).

This magnificent species is unique to North America. When fully mature, they measure over five feet tall (all necks and legs), with a wingspan of up to seven and a half feet. They have white feathers with black wing tips, and red and black heads. Courtship begins at the end of winter; whooping cranes mate for life and are famous for an elaborate courtship dance that consists of calling, flapping, tremendous jumping high in the air, and fervent head bowing.

Whooping cranes breed in northwestern Canada and migrate in groups of two to six to the refuge, 2,500 miles southeast. The birds arrive on the south Texas coast in late October and stay to nest until mid-March or April.

Early in this century, new towns and cities across U.S. territory changed the environment whooping cranes used for migration. The crane population dropped off and by 1941 the population had dwindled to sixteen. Scientists and wildlife officials increased the species' chance for survival by transferring eggs from whooper nests to the nests of sandhill cranes (a slightly smaller species) at Gray's Lake National

Wildlife Refuge in Idaho. The sandhill cranes, acting as foster parents, successfully raised the young chicks, adding twenty-five cranes to the world population, and the species has made a gradual but healthy comeback since.

Whooping cranes migrating to (above) *and feeding at* (below) *Aransas National Wildlife Refuge—a rare sight to behold.*
(Courtesy U.S. Department of the Interior)

The Lyndon B. Johnson Space Center

President John F. Kennedy furthered our nation's space program in 1961 by announcing his aspiration to place a man on the moon before the end of the decade. Within a few months, plans had been drawn up for the NASA (National Aeronautics and Space Administration) Space Task Group at Langley Research Center. Requirements in targeting a site for the center included convenience to water transport; proximity to a military base, a commercial jet airport, an established university specializing in science and space-related research, adequate water and energy supplies, a pool of contractor and industrial support, and a culturally active community; a major telecommunications network; a year-round mild climate; and at least four square kilometers for construction.

After a thorough investigation of possible sites around the country, a 1,620-acre site in Clear Lake City, twenty-five miles southeast of Houston, was chosen. It was later named in honor of Kennedy's successor.

On July 4, 1962, Houston hosted the largest parade and barbecue in its history to honor the arrival of the seven original astronauts: M. Scott Carpenter, L. Gordon Cooper, Jr., John H. Glenn, Jr., Virgil I. "Gus" Grissom, Walter M. Schirra, Jr., Alan B. Shepard, Jr., and Donald K. "Deke" Slayton. The space center opened in September 1963.

The first words transmitted to earth by Commander Neil Armstrong from Apollo 11 lunar lander on the surface of the moon in 1969 were: "Houston, Tranquility Base here. The Eagle has landed." He took man's first step onto the moon, with the words: "That's one small step for [a] man, one giant leap for mankind."

The center, which has 3,250 federal employees, among them eighty astronauts, develops, tests, and designs manned space-flight systems with a goal of one day developing a permanently manned space station. Astronauts are selected and trained to conduct experiments in engineering, medical, and scientific experiments in outer space. Both civilians and military personnel are considered for the one-year training program.

There are 100 buildings on site, and many are open to the public. The most popular attraction is the Mission Control Center. At Mission Control, all manned space flights are monitored after lift-off. When no mission is in operation, simulated flight conditions and events are used to train controllers and astronauts. Briefings for visitors last about thirty-five minutes, and tickets are available on a first-come, first-served basis. In the past, Mission Control has been closed to the public when an actual mission is under way; however, this policy may change as flights become more routine.

The Mission Simulation and Training Facility, used to prepare astronauts for Skylab missions, is another crowd-pleaser. Here you can see firsthand how astronauts live and work in space. The Lunar Sample Building houses almost 800 pounds of lunar material collected from the moon during six Apollo missions. The Mockup and Integration Laboratory contains a full-scale model of the orbiter's cabin and cargo bay station that you may enter.

Currently, NASA scientists, engineers, and technicians are developing the nation's first permanently manned space station. Human outposts are planned for the moon by 2005 and Mars by 2015.

You may tour by yourself or join a guided tour starting at 10:00 A.M. every day of the year (except Christmas). Tours are free. Call (713) 483-4321 for more information.

NASA's history is told by a display of spacesuits worn by American astronauts throughout the last three decades.
(Courtesy NASA)

NASA's space shuttle.
(Courtesy NASA)

The Astrodome:
Eighth Wonder of the World

The Houston Astrodome is the world's first all-weather, multipurpose stadium and has been used as a model for every indoor stadium constructed since. First opened in 1965, the Astrodome is the home of the Houston Astros (baseball), the Houston Oilers (football), and the University of Houston Cougars (football). Its less spectacular, official name is Harris County Domed Stadium. The complex covers 260 acres and has a seating capacity of 45,000 for baseball; 52,000 for football; 60,000 for conventions; and 66,000 for wrestling and boxing events. A $60 million expansion project will add thousands of seats, and a new "Magic Carpet," an artificial surface rolled out on a cushion of air, developed by Monsanto, will cover the playing field for both baseball and football. The Astrodome is the first stadium in the country to have two separate playing surfaces at its disposal, one for baseball and one for football.

The Astrodome's scoreboard is 474 feet long and four stories high, one of the largest in the world. It has a 26½-by-37½-foot high-tech instant-replay screen, and a "Home Run Spectacular" that wows audiences with an enthusiastic forty-second display to celebrate home runs: the "Spectacular" has over 40,000 tiny lights programmed to blink various images—cowboys riding, roping, and shooting; snorting bulls with flags on their horns; the Astrodome with a home-run ball exploding through the roof; fireworks. A company founded by George Lucas, creator of *Star Wars,* is planning a new show of special effects for the scoreboard.

The world's first completely air-conditioned stadium, the Astrodome boasts 6,600 tons of cooling capacity during each event, circulating 2.5 million cubic feet of fresh air per minute. Once, when the air-conditioning system was turned off, the condensation formed a raincloud and caused an unexpected indoor shower!

The roof of the Astrodome is clear, spanning 642 feet, twice that of any previous structure, and is 208 feet high—room for an eighteen-story building! The frame of the roof is a steel skeleton, sturdy enough to withstand hurricane winds up to 135 miles per hour.

The kilowatt-hours needed to illuminate the field are more than is required by a town with a population of 9,000, or roughly twice that currently required by Columbus, site of Stephen F. Austin's first settlement.

Tours of the Astrodome begin daily at 11:00 A.M. and 1:00 and 3:00 P.M., with an additional tour starting at 5:00 P.M. from June 1 through August 31. If any afternoon event is scheduled, only one tour, beginning at 10:00 A.M., is held. Call in advance to confirm the schedule: (713) 799-9544.

The Houston Astrodome: Eighth Wonder of the World.
(Courtesy Houston Astro Baseball Club)

The Dallas/Fort Worth Airport

Dallas/Fort Worth International Airport (DFW), the largest airport in the United States, seems more a city than an airport. It is so big that walking from terminal to terminal is almost impossible. Over 44 million passengers passed through the airport in 1988.

Passengers use Air Trans, an electric train system, for transportation between distant terminals. The electric train generally takes up to fifteen minutes between terminals, but traveling from terminal 2W on the west side (TWA and Pan Am) to 4E on the east side (Delta) takes thirty minutes. The trains are the only way to get from one terminal to another, and they have a 99-percent efficiency rate.

Open since 1974, DFW lies on 17,800 acres in Dallas and Tarrant counties. Thirteen boarding gates and over 675,000 aircraft operations, made this the third busiest airport in the world in 1988, after Atlanta International and Chicago's O'Hare.

DFW is proud to have the world's largest parking lot, with room enough to accommodate more than 27,000 vehicles—one space for each of the 26,000 airport employees, with a few to spare!

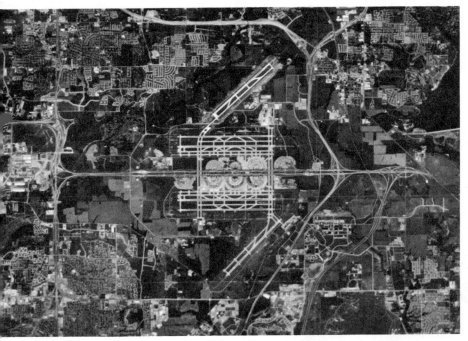

An aerial shot of the Dallas/Fort Worth Airport—almost a city in itself!
(Courtesy Dallas/Fort Worth International Airport Information Department)

Aquarena Springs

Aquarena Springs is an amusement park in San Marcos built on the freshwater springs of the San Marcos River. It offers unique underwater attractions, including rides in glass-bottomed boats.

The world's only submarine theater is located at Aquarena Springs. Graceful "aquamaids" perform intricate underwater jazz and ballet routines, and Ralph, a famous resident pig, shows off his trademark Swine Dive.

Aquarena Springs is open to all water fans throughout the year. Operating hours vary seasonally; for more information call (512) 396-8900.

The Ghost Squadron

"Ghosts" fly authentic World War II planes from the Confederate Air Force Flying Museum at Valley International Airport in Harlingen. The Ghost Squadron reminds us of many Americans' heroism, patriotism, and national purpose during the war. The museum has the finest and most complete collection of working World War II aircraft in the world; several planes are the last known surviving models. On display are 142 aircraft (61 different models), including Warhawks, Navy Cats, an A6M Zero, and a Flying Fortress, all restored to their original working order.

The most unusual exhibit at the museum is the only original collection of "nose art" in the world. Back in the war days, bomber crews painted pictures on their airplanes, usually lovely ladies or cartoon characters. Nose art is considered an original American art form.

In addition to the aircraft, there is an extensive collection of World War II memorabilia, consisting of more than 50,000 artifacts. From tanks to machine guns and handguns, almost every type of weapon used during the war is represented. There is also a display showing every type of American military medal, including the Medal of Honor, Distinguished Flying Cross, Silver Star, and Bronze Star. A comprehensive exhibit of uniforms represents many countries, including the U.S., Great Britain, France, Germany, Italy, Japan, and Poland.

The Flying Museum is open Monday through Saturday from 9:00 A.M. to 5:00 P.M. Hours on Sundays and holidays are 1:00 to 6:00 P.M. Call (512) 425-1057 for further information.

The River Walk

You don't have to travel to Paris or Venice to find sidewalk cafés and cabarets lining the banks of a beautiful river. Come to San Antonio's internationally known River Walk, and enjoy the tranquil beauty of brightly colored barges gliding over the water.

In 1921 a disastrous flood caused the horseshoe bend of the San Antonio River to overflow. A wall of water pushed into the streets of the downtown area, killing dozens of people and sweeping away large houses. To prevent a recurrence, concerned citizens wanted to fill the picturesque horseshoe bend with dirt. No river, no more floods.

A group of conservationists, however, wanted to save the city's beautiful river bend. The San Antonio Conservation Society urged city commissioners to spare the bend for future use. After much debate, a motion was made to cut the horseshoe bend off during heavy rainfall with a new bypass channel. A floodgate and two dams were built, and by 1929 a new channel was completed.

Robert Hugman, an architect who had spent his boyhood days fishing along the banks of the river, envisioned a world apart from the city's streets along the river. He suggested adding gondolas and constructed thirty-one stairways leading to the River Walk, each in a different design. Hugman also built an outdoor theater.

It wasn't until the 1960s that the riverfront was completely developed. A $30 million bond was issued in 1964 to improve the river bend. Now the area is a city park, complete with botanical gardens, dozens of boutiques, cafés, and an array of delightful entertainment. If you are ever in the mood for a romantic day, visit the River Walk and ride on one of the gondolas!

The First Columbus

Along the banks of the Colorado River, seventy miles west of Houston, sits a historic town where one of the first Anglo-American colonies in Texas was settled, in 1823. The tiny town of Columbus served as Stephen F. Austin's headquarters until Indian problems forced him to move.

In 1835 General Sam Houston camped east of the town, and Mexican army general Santa Anna followed, camping west of Columbus for five days. To keep Santa Anna from taking control of the town, Houston ordered it burned to the ground. The settlers fled eastward ahead of the Mexican forces. Not until the 1870s did Columbus grow and prosper again. Over twenty years of restoration work, research, and community spirit have brought back the days of Old Texas to tourists passing through Columbus.

Guided historic walking tours, held monthly by Magnolia Homes Tour group, take visitors through sixty famous homes and historic buildings. The Raumonda, today a beautiful bed-and-breakfast inn, is a classic example of symmetrical Greek revival architecture popular during the Victorian era. Built of cypress, with pine floors and woodwork, this historic landmark is filled with beautiful nineteenth-century antiques and includes a lavish formal garden.

The old courthouse, constructed of bricks made from Colorado River clay and sheltered by a magnificent stained-glass dome, is a sight to behold! Built in 1891 in the Second

59

Raumonda, a beautiful bed-and-breakfast inn, is a historic landmark in Columbus. (Courtesy Columbus Chamber of Commerce)

Empire style, it has been completely restored. Hand-carved newel posts and wainscoting of red heart pine are additional outstanding features. Daughters of the Republic of Texas in nineteenth-century costume greet visitors at a two-room log cabin complete with authentic furnishings. Built in 1836 by Abraham Alley, one of Stephen Austin's original colonists, it was located several miles below Columbus at the Atascosito Trail crossing of the Colorado River and was moved into the town in 1976. Alley's descendants donated the cabin and money for restoration to Magnolia Homes Tour. Very few authentic cabins exist from this period.

The Alley Log Cabin, built in 1836 by Abraham Alley, one of Stephen F. Austin's original colonists.
(Courtesy Columbus Chamber of Commerce)

*The old courthouse
of Columbus.*
(Courtesy Columbus
Chamber of
Commerce)

*The stained-glass dome
of the old courthouse.*
(Courtesy Columbus
Chamber of
Commerce)

The restored Stafford Opera House, built in 1886, hosted Lillian Russell, Al Jolson, and Harry Houdini, among others. Also included on the Magnolia tour are the Senftenberg-Brandon House, a Greek revival building from the 1880s and the 1860 Dilue Rose Harris House, of unique "tabby" construction.

Historic Columbus boasts many firsts. It was the site of the first Indian battle in Texas in 1823, as well as the first corn crop in the territory. The first Texas Rangers were organized there, in the summer of 1823. The first official election in Texas was held in Columbus, on August 16, 1823. The first formal Fourth of July celebration in Texas took place there in 1826, with a primitive barbecue on the banks of the Colorado River.

Columbus, with population under 5,000, is the oldest continuously occupied Anglo-American settlement in Texas and holds on fiercely to the memories of a bygone era. Visitors are welcomed with open arms and southern hospitality the big Texas way! If you are interested in taking the tour, call the Columbus Chamber of Commerce, (409) 732-5881. For bed-and-breakfast information or reservations, call (409) 732-3864.

Texas Nightlife

Texans have a reputation for entertaining themselves like no one else. Cowboy hats and boots may go with jeans or a tuxedo. Texans prefer "watering holes" to "bars," "music saloons" to "clubs," and "hoedown halls" to "discos." The huge parking lots adjacent to holes, saloons, and halls are as likely to be filled with all models of pickup trucks (many with gun racks) as with flashy sports cars.

Dallas Alley is a haven of shops, restaurants, and bars.
(Courtesy Dallas Convention & Visitors Bureau)

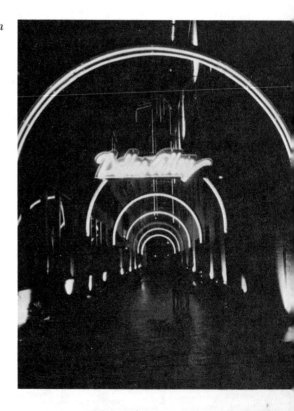

Gilley's

Once the most famous of all nightclubs in Texas, Gilley's found fame and fortune even before it was featured in the film *Urban Cowboy*. Located in Pasadena, a small town outside Houston, Gilley's was about the size of a football field. As many as 5,000 cowboys and cowgirls could fill the club to dance, kick, and drink the night away.

Gilley's was named for popular country-and-western singer Mickey Gilley, cousin of Jerry Lee Lewis. Gilley, a winner of the Academy of Country Music's Entertainer of the Year Award, also has a Grammy to his credit, which he won with his band, the Urban Cowboys, for "Orange Blossom Special Hoedown." He has hosted a radio show, *Live at Gilley's*, broadcast to over 300 stations in the United States.

Now Gilley's is a thing of the past. Described as the "biggest, brawlingest, dancingest, craziest honky-tonk in Texas," the nightclub was locked shut after a legal tussle between Gilley and onetime partner Sherwood Cryer. Gilley won a lawsuit to have his name removed from the club and received millions of dollars owed him. The club was in dire need of renovation and Gilley felt that its poor maintenance wasn't fairly representing his image.

Gilley's was famous for its live music—often big-name singers like Willie Nelson—and dancing, but it was also renowned for its electric bull. Toro, the most celebrated electric bull in the world, was a central player with John

Travolta and Debra Winger in *Urban Cowboy*. Originally designed to train bull riders for rodeo competitions, Toro became a popular source of nighttime entertainment. The 600-pound machine gyrated, bucked, and spun at various speeds, depending on the rider's skill. Mattresses and foam pads surrounded the bull to protect thrown riders. To be considered a very good rider, you had to remain on the bull, keep one hand high up above your head, and never let your hat fall off.

The club's popularity spawned custom T-shirts, sweat-shirts, beach towels, key chains, beer mugs, designer jeans, and even its own brand of beer. Unfortunately, it seems now that Gilley's has already seen its last roundup!

The Swingingest Laundromat
in the World

Holmes' Coin-O-Mat makes your washing and drying fun, in a way we've seen only in Texas. In Azle, sixteen miles northwest of Fort Worth, you can twist and spin with your laundry in an establishment decorated deceptively like any other laundromat.

The wash-and-dry is nothing special unless you opt to do your laundry on Friday nights. While most people would scoff at anyone who saves cleaning for weekend evenings, Holmes' Friday-night patrons enjoy rip-roaring free western music shows.

Since 1964 Holmes' Coin-O-Mat has offered this entertainment, attracting hundreds of country-music buffs. Most of the talent is amateur, although some performers are as good as guests who have appeared on *Hee Haw*. An evening of good, clean fun is what one will find at Holmes'—no smoking or drinking—and the whole family is welcome. People from around the world visiting the Fort Worth area tour up to Azle to hoedown at the cleaner's. If you're looking for new and different Friday-night fun, bring your dirty clothes on over, and have a good ol' time.

Miss Hattie's

At one time more than thirty-five saloons and bawdyhouses lined the streets of San Angelo; today you can't even purchase a bottle of liquor within the city limits. Miss Hattie's was one of those bawdyhouses; it is now an authentic bordello museum. Original furnishings, personal articles, and clothing are now on display in the house.

The waiting room and upstairs hallway at Miss Hattie's.
(Courtesy Miss Hattie's)

Miss Goldie's room, decorated entirely in gold tones—her favorite color.
(Courtesy Miss Hattie's)

Built in 1896, the prosperous brothel entertained
ranchers, cowboys, and soldiers in its heyday in the early
1900s. The Texas Rangers shut it down in 1946. There were
various owners during its fifty years in operation; Miss
Hattie acquired part ownership of the house in 1902 as a
divorce settlement, her ex-husband staying on to operate
the saloon on the first floor. Miss Hattie governed the upstairs, where she conducted a profitable business and kept a
number of consorts herself.

Still intact are catwalks for quick exits, and a warning light
and alarm bell used for police raids. The girls' bedrooms are

maintained exactly as they were decorated for gentlemen callers. Two notorious characters were Miss Blue, a star attraction, whose room is decorated accordingly, and Miss Rosie, who preferred red clothing and had a fire-engine-red room with an adjacent catwalk for clients' discreet departures.

An astute businesswoman, Miss Hattie had a house doctor and forbade her girls to drink alcohol. She also had the first indoor plumbing in town! After her retirement, she lived quietly until her death in 1982, at the age of 104.

Miss Hattie's is open for tours from 10:00 A.M. to 3:30 P.M. Tuesday through Saturday. Call (915) 655-2518 for further information.

Is That a Chicken in Your Pocket, or Are You Just Glad to See Me?

In its day, the Chicken Ranch, a house of ill repute in La Grange, was one of the state's main attractions—a real Texas institution. In 1910 the sheriff of this otherwise sleepy small town personally selected a new location for hardworking resident girls, and the brothel was moved from atop the local hardware store to a sedate rural setting on the outskirts of town. The establishment enjoyed such popularity that many of the boys who frequented the house during World War I loyally sent their sons for a visit during World War II.

Only during the Depression did the Chicken Ranch have a spell of slow business. It wasn't always easy to come up with hard cash, so for a while the girls began accepting poultry for their services. Not long thereafter it was dubbed the Chicken Ranch.

In 1973 Marvin Zindler, a Houston consumer advocate, led a fierce campaign that eventually closed the ranch. But its memory lives on—the Chicken Ranch inspired the hit Broadway musical *The Best Little Whorehouse in Texas*, made into a movie starring Burt Reynolds and Dolly Parton.

71

Texas Ladies Aside

The Texas Ladies Aside drill team, who ride sidesaddle on horseback, is the only such team in the nation. Members ride only good-tempered Peruvian horses in order to accentuate their femininity and showmanship.

Being part of a precision drill team is time-consuming and expensive. Members live across Texas, and many travel hundreds of miles for practice sessions.

Since 1983 Texas Ladies Aside have appeared at parades and exhibitions all over Texas. The team performs at the Cotton Bowl, the Fort Worth Stock Show, and the National Show for Peruvian Horses in Lima. Each March they are featured at the Caldwell Spring Festival. Each summer they conduct a weekend workshop, "Introduction to Sidesaddle."

The Texas Ladies Aside team, outfitted in bright red cowboy skirts and blouses, is accompanied by Men Besides, male escorts who wear stark white and carry flags.

The Rodeo

The legendary cowboy is a symbol by which the United States is recognized. Today, tradition and heritage are most visibly exemplified by the professional rodeo cowboy. He competes in a sport that sprang directly out of his forebears' daily work.

The history of rodeo dates back more than a century. As settlers traveled west into the frontier, the American cowboy was born, first as a hired hand on horseback. While tending the cattle, cowboys challenged each other to show off their riding skills. Contests soon evolved with saddle bronc riding, team roping, and calf roping as games of choice. These contests moved from the pastures to the towns, where they became spectator sport. In parts of Texas, professional rodeos are more popular than the movies.

Many professionals begin rodeoing at very young ages. Minor-league ranking begins with Little Britches for elementary school–aged children, and continues to Junior High, High School, Intercollegiate, and amateur competitions. It is not uncommon for a contestant to have competed in over fifty rodeos before entering a professional event. A great many of today's professionals attended a rodeo school conducted by professionals as they pursued various league levels. The caliber of rodeo competition runs very high.

The Professional Rodeo Cowboys Association sanctions about 650 rodeos a year, and chances are, there's always a rodeo in progress in Texas. Professional cowboys lead a tough life, touring through a grinding eleven-month schedule and always risking injury.

World champion in both bareback and saddle bronc events is thirty-two-year-old Lewis Field, a native Texan. He has won three consecutive all-around titles (1986, 1987, and 1988) and has made quite a successful career on the professional rodeo circuit. His 1988 winnings totaled over $75,000 not including promotional and advertising work.

Rodeos have found a prominent place in American sports. Now more than just a rough-and-tumble event, they have become a popular way to raise money for charities and communities. With so many to choose from, you cannot afford to miss a fun-filled night at the rodeo, Texas style!

The Mesquite Championship Rodeo

Just fifteen minutes or so from Dallas, is Mesquite, home of a rodeo guaranteed to keep its patrons on the edge of their seats. The Mesquite Championship Rodeo is a major tourist attraction, Texas's biggest and most popular rodeo, featuring bull riders, sharpshooters, calf ropers, daredevil clowns, and steer wrestlers. Pony rides and the Kiddie Korral Barnyard and Calf Scramble let young cowpokes get into the action.

The rodeo's roughest and most dangerous characters are the high-tempered bucking bulls of the Mesquite Arena. Bulls averaging 1,800 pounds, with well-earned names like Spotted Fever, Wipe Out, and Red Alert, are terrors to riders, who are required to stay on for at least eight seconds.

Cowboys Neal Gay and Jim Shoulders corralled their famous colleagues in 1958 to participate in the Mesquite Rodeo. Gay led a long career on the professional rodeo circuit, leading in events such as saddle bronc, bareback, bull riding, and steer wrestling. Since his retirement, he remains active as a rodeo producer; his three sons have become professional cowboys. One of them, Don, won a record-setting eight bull-riding titles; he has retired from competition and is now vice-president of the Mesquite Arena.

The rodeo runs from April through September, with events held every Friday and Saturday night. The Mesquite Arena is an all-weather facility with an indoor seating capacity of 6,000. Televised broadcasts of the rodeo, aired on The Nashville Network, boast very high ratings. The Old West lives on at the Mesquite Championship Rodeo!

The Mesquite Championship Rodeo is televised to over 2 million households across the country. (Photo by Mike Blacker)

The San Angelo Stock Show
and Rodeo

The San Angelo Stock Show and Rodeo Association hosts many different events throughout the year, among the most popular a quarterhorse division, a premium stock show, a genuine rodeo, and a world championship goat-roping contest.

The goat-roping contest in May attracts professional goat-ropers from across the country. Sixty ropers compete for the fastest time in tying up a Spanish goat. Contestants on horseback rope the goat before dismounting; then they must wind the rope around three legs of the animal and pin it down while an official makes an examination.

In March the San Angelo Invitational Ranch Rodeo, representing eleven Texas counties, pits teams of ten cowboys against each other in a series of events. Only legitimate, full-time cowboys from local ranches may enter. Each man uses his own horse, and official rules state that each competitor must be dressed in full ranch-cowboy regalia (chaps, boots, spurs, long-sleeved shirt, cowboy hat). Regular events include horse catching, bronc riding, team branding, and cow milking.

The San Angelo Stock Show, held each March since 1932, features prime stock lambs, steers, and junior barrows. Sixty-four choice lambs and eighteen selected steers, including the grand champions and runners-up from the livestock show, are on the market at the stock show's premium sale. Some of the highest-quality stock in the country is shown at the San Angelo Stock Show.

Western activities of all types fill San Angelo's schedule year-round, from champion quarterhorse, lamb, and steer shows to the rodeo of genuine cowboys who still rope and ride the rough way. Here is a genuine piece of American history and culture definitely not to be missed.

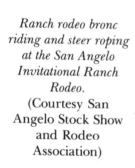

Ranch rodeo bronc riding and steer roping at the San Angelo Invitational Ranch Rodeo.
(Courtesy San Angelo Stock Show and Rodeo Association)

The XIT Ranch

Located in the western Texas Panhandle, the XIT Ranch was once the largest range in the world under fence. It extended some 3,050,000 acres and sprawled across what are now portions of ten counties. In 1879 the 16th Texas Legislature agreed to barter this large parcel for the construction of a capitol building. A bargain was struck with two Chicago contractors who agreed to erect a $3.2 million capitol in exchange for the ranch.

In 1885 the first cattle were brought to the XIT Ranch. In 1900, its heyday, the ranch handled 150,000 cattle, had 335 windmills, 94 different pastures, and 7 headquarter stations. Fifteen hundred miles of barbed-wire fence surrounded the ranch. About a year after the ranch hit its peak, the owners started selling off tracts of land in an effort to begin dissolving the partnership, and by 1929 the last of the cattle were gone. The corrals, foreman's house, and bunkhouse still stand at Buffalo Springs, thirty-two miles north of Dalhart.

The famous XIT brand for which the ranch is named was developed by veteran cowboy Abner Blocker; these letters were simple to produce on a branding iron and were large and difficult to alter by rustlers. The brand is just the capital letters X, I, and T, with the I a single vertical line. In one of Texas's most famous rustling stories, a band of thieves stole a herd of cattle and disguised the XIT brand as a six-pointed star.

79

Dalhart is also the home of the XIT Museum, which features a turn-of-the-century parlor, bedroom, and kitchen; a pioneer chapel used by XIT ranch hands; and a real chuckwagon, once used to prepare meals for XIT ranchers working out on the range.

Tour hours are 2:00 to 5:00 P.M. Tuesday through Saturday and the first Sunday of each month. Call (806) 249-5390 for further information.

The King Ranch

The King Ranch, near Kingsville, is one of the world's largest operating cattle and horse ranches. The biggest ranch in Texas, it sprawls over more than 1,300 square miles (825,000 square acres), which makes it larger than the entire state of Rhode Island (which measures 1,214 square miles). The ranch is surrounded by 2,000 miles of fence, almost enough to stretch from Kingsville to Boston, and has 2,730 oil wells and 350 windmills for pumping water. The Kingsville ranch, whose brand represents running water, is also home to 60,000 Santa Gertrudis cattle and 1,000 registered quarterhorses.

The King Ranch is the birthplace of the American ranching business. In 1852 Captain Richard King stumbled upon the Santa Gertrudis Creek, his first sighting of water after traveling on horseback through the Wild Horse Desert to the Long Star State Fair, some 124 miles. King and a friend of his, Captain Gideon K. "Legs" Lewis of the Texas Rangers, formed a partnership to establish and operate a livestock operation with headquarters at the creek. King purchased the land and began his long battle to conquer the desert and his neighbors, the Apaches.

After the Civil War, more than 100,000 head of King Ranch cattle were distributed throughout the nation, as food and as stock for hundreds of ranches. The King Ranch developed the first American beef breed and produced

81

some of the all-time top running and performance horses. The ranch developed its own breed of cattle, the Santa Gertrudis, a cross of Indian Brahman and British short-horn. This breed can endure the hot, dry Texas climate without expensive, extra care and can still provide lean quality beef. The ranch now produces 25,000 beef calves a year.

The King Ranch champion quarterhorse program began in 1915, when Bob Kleberg, King's grandson, bought Old Sorrel, a colt that became the foundation sire that made the ranch famous. Old Sorrel was bred with many top mares and produced excellent offspring.

In 1940 the American Quarter Horse Association was founded. The board agreed that the number-one quar-terhorse in the stud book would be the grand champion of the 1941 Fort Worth Fat Stock Show. The champion was King Ranch's Wimpy, grandson of Old Sorrel. Success fol-lowed success as the King Ranch continued to put more enthusiasm into all of its horse programs.

In 1974 the ranch purchased a phenomenal cutting-horse stallion. Cutting horses are trained to work with herds of cattle, "cutting" the cattle to keep them in line and moving in the right direction. Coincidentally, the stallion, named Mr. San Peppy, was a direct descendant of Old Sorrel. He won the 1972 National Cutting Horse Association (NCHA) Derby and was the open world Champion in 1974 and 1976. Mr. San Peppy was also world cutting champion of the American Quarter Horse Association in 1976 and thus was the first horse to win both world titles in the same year. He was also the first horse to win over $100,000 in open cutting competition and the youngest to be inducted into the NCHA Hall of Fame. Mr. San Peppy's son Peppy San Badger (Little Peppy) also won countless competitions, and he is the pre-mier sire in cutting today. His offspring have continued the

King Ranch tradition of excellence, as they have been strong contenders in every major competition. Of twenty horses competing in the finals of the 1985 NCHA Futurity, five were sired by Little Peppy. In the 1986 competition, eleven of the top forty-two horses were Little Peppy's offspring, including the reserve open champion and the open champion gelding. That's a strong Texas gene pool!

Today the King Ranch is a modern, diversified corporation whose stockholders are virtually all descendants of Captain Richard King. A multinational livestock corporation, the ranch controls more than 4 million acres worldwide, on which a variety of products are raised—sugar cane, cotton, sweet corn, in addition to cattle.

There is a lot more to learn about the King Ranch by seeing it firsthand. Take a tour of the ranch on the loop road, which takes you around the grounds. Call (512) 592-6411 for more information.

The Cadillac Ranch

The Cadillac Ranch is an unforgettable sight. Located on the outskirts of Amarillo and visible from U.S. Route 66 are ten Cadillacs, apparently sprouting out of the Texas prairie, flashy tailfins stretching toward the sky.

What you see is a permanent work of art placed on the 32,000-acre ranch of an eccentric man named Stanley Marsh 3. In 1974 Marsh, a successful local TV station owner and entrepreneur, commissioned the Ant Farm, an imaginative architectural designing firm in San Francisco, to build the Cadillac Ranch. When the Ant Farm was done, ten Cadillacs were forever buried nosedown into Texas soil, resting on concrete anchors. The automobiles lean west at a forty-five-degree angle, the same as the slope of the Great Pyramids. Each model reflects a change in tailfin style from 1948 through 1964, when the fin craze faded.

Why was the Cadillac chosen as Marsh's theme? Because he wanted to do something commemorating the generation of his youth. In the fifties the Cadillac reached a pinnacle of styling leadership—the bigger the fin, the better. General Motors' advertising campaign brazenly declared its elite Cadillac as the "standard of the world." In a society where the automobile is the chief status symbol, the owner of a Cadillac was in a class by himself. Other car companies looked to Caddys as a standard of quality against which to measure their own products.

The glorious fifties are commemorated in the "Stonehenge of Texas" at the Marsh ranch. (Courtesy Stanley Marsh 3)

Marsh considers his Cadillac Ranch "serious art" but allows, "It's humorous and just plain fun. What's more, it fits into my theory of art that all art should be valueless. It's nonmovable, so you can't really sell the Cadillac Ranch for anything. How can you when it's firmly cemented into the ground?"

Marsh points out that his sculpture has more cultural value than you'd expect at first. "It's one of the most amazing pieces of sculpture in the twentieth century. Someday it will be the Stonehenge and the thing that everyone remembers."

The Big Texan Steak Ranch

The Big Texan Steak Ranch restaurant in Amarillo is known coast to coast for its seventy-two-ounce-steak dinner. If you can finish one within an hour, your meal is on the house.

Once your dinner has been served, you are not permitted to leave the table if you want to walk away without a tab. Your plate must be clean, which means polishing off not only a gigantic steak, but also a shrimp cocktail, a baked potato, salad, and a roll. Of course, you don't have to eat the fat, but judges decide what is to be consumed and what isn't. Close to 22,000 have attempted to meet the challenge since it started in 1963, but only 3,500 men and 400 women have rolled out scot-free. If you are unsuccessful, you must shell out $29.95 before you can leave! The Big Texan also offers western delicacies such as buffalo steaks and hamburgers, rabbit, rattlesnake, and calf fries.

Adjacent to the restaurant you will find an Old West–style motel, a Texas-shaped swimming pool, a shooting gallery, a trading post, and a collection of Indian artifacts and wild animal trophies.

The folks at the Big Texan say, "Our Texas brand of hospitality will warm your heart—and bust your belt!"

Finish this seventy-two-ounce-steak dinner, and it's on the house.
(Courtesy Big Texan Steak Ranch)

The Governor's Mansion

The Texas Governor's Mansion is one of the most stately government residences in the nation. Home to thirty-six governors and their families since 1856, it has survived the ravages of the Civil War and occupation by Yankee soldiers.

In 1854, when Austin was a sparsely populated town of 3,000, the state legislature authorized $16,500 for the construction and decoration of a residence for the governor. Of that, $14,000 was allotted for construction costs, and the rest was set aside for interior furnishings—huge sums back then. Andrew Jackson's famous Nashville home, The Hermitage, was the chosen architectural model, and the interior was furnished and decorated in simple Texas frontier style.

Six white fluted columns rise twenty-nine feet to a balcony on the second story, which extends the full width of the house. Only two rooms have been added since the original construction: a kitchen wing and a family dining room, constructed in 1914.

The first occupants were the Elisha Marshall Pease family, who moved in on June 14, 1856. The house remained unchanged until Governor Sam Houston moved in with his wife and eight children and built a partition between two bedrooms, creating a much needed extra bedroom.

The house was sparsely furnished, and many rooms remained bare during the nineteenth century. Most of the present furnishings were privately contributed with the ap-

The Texas Governor's Mansion.
(Photo by Jack Lewis, *Texas Highways* magazine)

proval of the Board of Mansion Supervisors, who monitor all changes and redecorating. The Texas Governor's Mansion is recognized as one of the finest examples of antebellum architecture in America and has earned a place in the National Register of Historic Places.

Southfork Ranch

Everyone knows Southfork as the glitzy estate featured in television's *Dallas*. Lorimar Productions uses the 8,000-square-foot, five-bedroom ranch house located in Plano, north of Dallas, for many of the most dramatic scenes each season. Formerly the Duncan Ranch, Southfork boasts an eighteen-story-high working oil rig. The visitors' tour covers the interior of the Ewing mansion, J.R.'s dressing room, and, during location filming, a chance to mingle with *Dallas* cast and crew. A tram will take you around the expansive ranch. The Southfork Museum displays mementos of the show, as well as a fan-boggling collection of memorabilia including props and fabulous costumes worn in past seasons' episodes.

Dallas epitomizes the wealth and glamour of a Texas oil family, the Ewings. Now a hit overseas, the show has been a huge boost to tourism in Dallas. People come from all over the world wondering if Texans really live like the Ewings. Southfork is open to the public every day from 9:00 A.M. to dusk. Who knows—you might even bump into J.R.

Southfork Ranch, of Dallas *fame.*
(Courtesy Dallas Convention & Visitors Bureau and Southfork Ranch)

The Beer Can House

Have we got a house for beer lovers! Houston's beer can house has been featured on dozens of television shows and in *Ripley's Believe It or Not.*

John M. Milkovisch and his wife, Mary, purchased a house from his father in 1941. In 1968 young Milkovisch, a former employee of Southern Pacific Railroad, began decorating his patio with brass, marbles, rocks, and buttons. Rather than cut the grass, he covered his lawn in the same fashion, and finished by embedding marbles into his redwood fence.

His obsession took a left turn when he began to collect old beer cans, flattening them to make sheets of aluminum siding. Dozens of can ends and pull tops were attached in long streamers to make curtains. The curtains in the windows glitter in the sunlight and chime whenever the wind blows. Says Milkovisch: "The art students come here and call it art. They try to put me in the same category as a sculptor, but I say, 'No way.' This curtain idea is just one of those dreams in the back of my noodle!"

The infamous beer can house. (Courtesy Mary Milkovisch)

A Princely Home . . .
at a Prince's Ransom

In spite of a recent real estate slump in Houston, one princely estate is on the market—for a mere $35 million. It is thus the most expensive listed residence in the world.

Owner Prince Abduli Faisal of Saudi Arabia built his "palace" in 1985. The 22,400 square feet of living space are given to twenty rooms, ten bathrooms, and five half-baths with gold-plated fixtures. Three recreation rooms are available for entertaining; one is a fully equipped gymnasium.

Built of imported white French limestone, Prince Faisal's home presides over three acres of beautifully maintained grounds and boasts a 60-by-22-foot swimming pool.

In the Texas style of living . . . bigger is *always* better.

Texas Money

Big Texas money was first made when the huge oil fields at Spindletop and Kilgore started producing incredible amounts of oil. Thousands of Texans benefited from the big gushers; rich oil fields promised a bright future. Where else but in Texas would you expect to find highways paved with real gold? His-and-hers Christmas presents worth over $2 million? A house for sale with a price tag of $35 million? A private airport with golf and tennis facilities and gourmet food? A cab company that uses only Cadillacs, each with a pair of longhorn horns on its front hood!

Striking It Rich at Spindletop

Beaumonters gave the name Spindletop to a field just on the outskirts of town, after the scrubby, spindly pines growing there. Petroleum vapors seeped through the soil in the field, and youngsters often went to light matches and ignite small flames. Grown-ups thought little of barren land where their cattle could not graze, never once considering the natural resources hidden beneath the surface. Oil was thought to exist only in places like Pennsylvania, *never* out west. One Standard Oil executive declared: "I'll drink any drop of oil west of the Mississippi."

Patillo Higgins, a Beaumont resident, was the first to guess that oil *was* indeed under Spindletop, and he invested $30,000 of his own money and $17,000 borrowed from friends to test-drill. By December 31, 1900, he had made a hole in the ground 1,020 feet deep, boring through an estimated 140 feet of solid rock. Discouraged at not having a windfall to celebrate the new year, Higgins and his crew called it quits and headed home. But on January 10, 1901, a geyser of oil suddenly shot out of the ground, spurting higher and higher, thus confirming the word *gusher* in the English vocabulary.

Soon the first of many Spindletop gushers was producing 100,000 barrels of oil a day, approximately sixty percent of total U.S. oil production. Another Spindletop well brought an amount equal to the combined total produced by 37,000 wells Standard Oil operated back east. Spindletop's first six holes produced 136 million barrels of oil in one year, more than double the output in Russia, the world's foremost petroleum producer at the time.

Practically overnight, Beaumont was transformed from a small, obscure town into an oil center with a population of over 50,000. Local landowners became millionaires by selling off land and leasing oil rights for an astronomical $100,000 per acre. Shopkeepers complained that customers never had smaller than thousand-dollar bills. Drinking water was so scarce that while oil was bringing in three cents a barrel, enterprising businessmen were selling water for six dollars a barrel.

Spindletop . . . a gusher that once produced sixty percent of the nation's oil.
(Courtesy Ann Lee & Associates)

With the discovery of oil at Spindletop, gasoline replaced kerosene as the primary source of fuel in America: oil became king. Three barrels of oil have the heating capacity of a ton of coal; not only is oil cleaner but it can be transported with considerably less effort. In the past, it took 100 men several days to load a ship with coal; now a single man could do the same task with oil in a matter of hours. Most important, the discovery of oil at Spindletop made our country the most powerful nation in the world. In the aftermath of World War I, the first war in which oil was used, it was said that the Allies "floated to victory on a wave of oil" while Germany's defeat was due to its petroleum deficiency.

When you are in Beaumont, be sure to stop in the Spindletop Museum, where you will find artifacts of the era, along with the documents and letters of early oilmen. It is open from 1:00 to 5:00 P.M. Monday through Friday. Call (409) 838-8896 for further details.

The World's Richest Acre

In 1930 wildcatter Columbus Marion ("Dad") Joiner discovered a rich oil field in Kilgore, a small town in east Texas. On December 19, he drilled a hole on the Daisy Bradford farm that soon became the richest oil well discovered since Spindletop started gushing near Beaumont.

A few months later, another well blew on a farm nine miles away; oil flowed here at a rate of 22,000 barrels a day. News of the success spread quickly around Texas, and 5,000 wildcatters rushed to the scene of the biggest boom in Texas history.

Joiner had found the richest oil field in the continental United States, but unfortunately he did not secure airtight leases before he started drilling. An Oklahoma poker player named H. L. Hunt offered help and financed Dad's operation. Hunt gave Dad $50,000 in cash, $45,000 in banknotes, and $1.3 million in future earnings.

The production rate in the Kilgore area was rapid. In the beginning seven wells were built every two weeks, then seven a day, until over a hundred wells were built daily. By July 1931, eleven hundred wells lined the streets of Kilgore. In August the National Guard had to be called into the area to keep peace among roughnecks, oil speculators, and wildcatters, all hoping for instant wealth promised by the rich fields. The success of the wells created the world's first billionaire, H. L. Hunt, but Dad Joiner lost his fortune in a real estate gamble and died a poor man in 1947.

Once the center of the Texas oil industry, with hundreds of working wells, Kilgore is now a quiet town. In total, the wells produced over 4.5 billion barrels of oil, and some are still pumping today. The world's richest acre is now part of the downtown area.

The East Texas Oil Museum at Kilgore College offers fascinating re-creations of town life during the early 1930s: wildcatters drill in fields, and townspeople work in a barbershop, post office, newspaper office, and general store. Also displayed are several tools actually used in the oil fields. Museum hours are 9:00 A.M. to 4:00 P.M. Tuesday through Saturday, and 2:00 to 5:00 P.M. on Sunday. Call (214) 983-8295 for more information.

The world's richest acre . . . center of the Texas oil industry.
(Courtesy Kilgore Chamber of Commerce)

Highways Paved with Gold

In 1936, while U.S. Highways 81 and 287 were being paved in Montague County in northern Texas, crews noticed that the sand used in the concrete glistened in the sun. Laboratory analysis in Fort Worth proved the sand was speckled with gold. At the time, its net worth of only fifty-four cents per ton made it unprofitable to extract the gold from the sand. The value of gold is substantially higher today than it was in 1936, and the gold that now spreads over thirty-nine miles of highways would be worth over a million dollars today.

The Neiman Marcus
Christmas Book

Neiman Marcus, one of the nation's most fashionable department stores, is headquartered in Dallas. The first U.S. department store to offer weekly fashion shows, it is known for flying a salesperson, armed with furs, haute couture dresses, and jewels, to an interested customer. There are now about a dozen Neiman Marcus stores across the country.

Neiman Marcus is perhaps best known for its Christmas Book, a catalogue full of gift suggestions that can be purchased exclusively from Neiman's. The catalogue, begun in 1915, is now distributed to 3.2 million clients worldwide and has a reputation for offering unusual gifts. In 1959 it featured a Black Angus steer, delivered alive on the hoof, or dead in steaks. A Neiman Marcus chocolate Monopoly set was Hugh Hefner's Christmas gift from his daughter one year. During the 1970 economic recession, the catalogue offered a modern-day Noah's Ark: for $588,247 you could have your own ark, complete with a Swedish masseur, German hairstylist, and English valet, Italian couturier, and French chef. In 1978 a $150,000 lynx coat was ordered by an elderly woman who wished to be buried in it.

The catalogue's famous His and Her Christmas gifts cater to the Texan who has everything and wishes to give surprising, original gifts year after year. Each his-and-her gift is carefully selected for quality, beauty, humor, and novelty.

Gifts suggested for Christmas 1960 were matching Beechcraft airplanes. Eight Chinese junks could be ordered in 1962. In 1968 the his gift was a Jaguar XKE grand-touring coupe, the hers a jaguar coat.

The his-and-her gifts (and not only these) are exorbitantly priced: among the items offered for couples in 1985 were diamonds for a total of $2 million. Over the years, the Christmas Book has also offered:

1963	His and Her Submarine	$18,700
1967	His and Her Camels	$ 4,125
1971	His and Her Mummy Cases (mummy included)	$16,000
1974	2-person Hoverbug marine vehicle	$ 3,640
1975	His and Her Dinosaur Safari in Utah	$29,995 each
1982	His and Her LaserTour exercise station	$20,000 each
1988	His and Her Cloudhopper hot-air balloon	$18,000

The ultimate Christmas gift... the his-and-her submarine from Neiman-Marcus. (Courtesy Neiman Marcus)

Aloft in the his-and-her hot-air balloon—a Christmas gift beyond compare!
(Courtesy Neiman Marcus)

During the Depression, a Texas oilman purchased an entire window display with a variety of gifts, from lingerie to a white ermine evening wrap. Neiman Marcus's owner, Stanley Marcus, had personally served the millionaire without success until he showed him the window display, which Neiman Marcus replicated secretly in the customer's home on Christmas Eve.

In 1988 *Time* and *Fortune* featured articles by George Plimpton about gift-giving. Plimpton challenged Neiman Marcus to come up with creative gift ideas for noted celebrities. The store thought the perfect gift for Katharine Hepburn, known for favoring turtleneck sweaters, would be a "parfait" of cashmere sweaters in various colors, presented in a giant brandy snifter and topped with a beautiful red ruby as the cherry. Plimpton loved the idea and purchased it for Hepburn.

A Millionaire's Million Air

Texas millionaires expect the best of everything, and they usually get it. Begun in 1984, Million Air is an exclusive private jet and helicopter charter service for those who want to receive red-carpet treatment when traveling by air to and from North Dallas.

Million Air facilities differ from those of other airlines: elaborate conference rooms, billiard rooms, gourmet catering services, a limousine service for door-to-aircraft convenience, even a modern health club, with members' privileges to nearby golf and tennis clubs. Pilots may enjoy luxury accommodations while they wait for their VIP passengers, and portable beepers alert the pilots when the passengers are ready to leave.

Million Air has proved so successful that it has developed into a franchise operation. There are now twenty-six Million Air facilities throughout North America, three of them in Texas, each with immediate participation by 1,700 aircraft. Owned by Richard R. Rogers, Chairman of Mary Kay Cosmetics, Inc., Million Air plans to have a total of thirty-two facilities by 1990.

The Texans!

Somehow, when a Texan comes up in conversation, *tall* is the first word that comes to mind. There is an old joke about a Texan walking down the streets of New York. A New Yorker points out the Empire State Building and the Texan says, "Son, I got news for you. Down in Texas, I got an outhouse bigger 'n that!" Obviously, Texans come in all shapes and sizes, but they can't shake their reputation for having an overabundance of state pride.

There are historical examples of colorful Texans who are most likely responsible for starting the belief that people from Texas are a vastly different species.

Stephen F. Austin

Born in Virginia in 1793 and raised in Missouri, Stephen F. Austin is considered the "Father of Texas." Austin's father, Moses, struck a deal in 1820 with the Mexican government to start a 300-family southwestern colony, but died a few months afterward. Although initially unenthusiastic about the project, Austin was moved by his dying father's last wish for him to pick up where the elder Austin was leaving off. Stephen dutifully assumed his father's role and started Texas's first settlement, in late 1821, along the coast of the Gulf of Mexico. A few years later, he imported 750 more families to Texas from the North. Austin mapped the land, started towns, schools, and legal systems. He went to great lengths to ensure that his settlers were both literate and industrious. After the last of his contracted colonists arrived, however, a wave of immigrants surged in and he could no longer monitor the character of the people moving to Texas. While some new arrivals were criminals escaping the law, most were common folk in search of a better life.

A strict Mexican government forced Austin to take an oath of allegiance to Mexico when he undertook the colonization of Texas. The colonists soon decided they wanted independence and sent Austin to Mexico City to negotiate secession from the Mexican government. Afraid that Texas would join the United States if it were a separate state, the Mexicans judged Austin a revolutionary and jailed him from 1834 to 1835.

Upon his release, Austin returned to Texas, now a republic, and ran for president. He lost to Sam Houston and was
appointed secretary of state, but died of natural causes soon
after at age forty-three.

Sam Houston

Considered its greatest statesman, Sam Houston served Texas as commander in chief of its first army, as president of the Republic of Texas, as U.S. senator from Texas, and finally as first governor of the state.

Born in Virginia on March 2, 1793, he moved to a farm in Tennessee when his mother was widowed in 1807. As a youngster, Houston occasionally lived with the Cherokee Indians of Tennessee and became an adopted son of Chief John Jolly, who christened him Raven. In the 1830s, during his trading days with the Arkansas Cherokee, he also became known as "Big Drunk."

At twenty-one, Houston enlisted in the Tennessee Regulars to fight in the Creek Indian War, under the command of General Andrew Jackson. During the climactic Battle of Horseshoe Bend, Houston was wounded several times by musket shots and arrows. The wounds never healed properly, and Houston would wear bandages the rest of his life.

In 1818 Houston, now a lawyer, became a Tennessee congressman; he served for two terms and was later elected governor. In 1832 he was sent to Texas by President Jackson to deliver a message to the Comanche Indians. Houston immediately fell in love with Texas. While in Austin, he was asked to lead the colonists in their revolt against the Mexican government. He was made commander in chief of the small Texas army gathered to fight for independence against the

Mexicans. In 1836 he led the army to victory over the Mexicans at San Jacinto and was voted president of the Republic of Texas; he was reelected in 1841.

Through Houston's influence, Texas chose to join the United States in 1845. Houston was a U.S. Senator from 1846 to 1859 and governor of the state from 1859 until the outbreak of the Civil War. He was removed from office for refusing to declare loyalty to the Confederacy, and he retired from public service. Houston died of pneumonia in 1863.

The Alamo—
A Shrine to Texas Liberty

Now a symbol of Texas liberty, the Alamo is the most visited site in Texas. Begun around 1756, the tranquil Spanish mission was originally called San Antonio de Valero. To all the world it is now the Alamo. (The Spanish *álamo* refers to a small poplar or cottonwood tree; a single cottonwood once shaded the spot where the landmark now stands.)

In its heyday, the Alamo resembled a small town, containing living quarters to house more than 300 Indians, a chapel, friary, farm, granary, textile and blacksmith shops, tannery, and stone-lined irrigation ditches. The main building has since been damaged; its walls have crumbled and the space within the mission has become a shady plaza. But to Texans it is still sacred soil.

On March 6, 1836, William B. Travis and his band of over 180 brave men fought and perished for Texas's independence. Among his group, for the most part volunteers, were Davy Crockett, noted frontiersman and statesman from Tennessee, and Jim Bowie, reputed inventor of the bowie knife. The small troop of dedicated, brave men knew death was imminent but were willing to give their lives rather than surrender their independence.

Four thousand Mexican troops under the command of General Santa Anna overwhelmed the Texans, attacking at daybreak, while the Texans were asleep. Still in a daze, the soldiers sprang to their posts. The Mexican troops quickly won entrance into the fortress, and a fierce battle followed. The battle lasted only ninety minutes; the Texans put up a valiant fight, but the Mexicans killed every one of them. The Mexican dead numbered around 1,600, according to Texans.

After his victory, Santa Anna celebrated in San Antonio. He then began a search for his rival, Sam Houston. Santa Anna found Houston and a small army of 800 Texans at the San Jacinto River. Or, rather, Houston found him. While the Mexican army set up camp and rested, Houston's troops swooped down on them, crying, "Remember the Alamo!" and killed over 600 Mexicans. Santa Anna was captured and his army surrendered. His remaining troops left behind at the Alamo quickly scattered.

Only two of the Alamo's original buildings remain today: a chapel, which displays memorabilia of the battle and the men who fought there, and a long barracks, once living quarters for priests and later soldiers, where an audiovisual presentation and two dioramas re-creating the final hours of the siege are offered.

The Alamo is open daily. Hours Monday through Saturday are 9:00 A.M. to 5:30 P.M., and Sunday 10:00 A.M. to 5:30 P.M.

The Texas Rangers

Contrary to popular opinion, the most famous Texas Rangers are not a professional baseball team. The real Texas Rangers are the oldest state law enforcement agency in North America. In 1823, as Texas was first being colonized, ten men armed with Colt revolvers, rifles, and bowie knives volunteered to protect the settlers of Texas from Indian raids and horse thieves. The Texas Ranger force exists today as part of the Texas Department of Public Safety, with ninety-four men under the direct command of Senior Ranger Captain H. R. Block.

It is said that these tough, shrewd men, considered the best fighting men around, could "ride like Mexicans, track like Comanches, shoot like Kentuckians, and fight like the devil."

Texas and Mexico had many disputes over territory, which led to war when Texas joined the Union in 1845. General Zachary Taylor led troops across the Rio Grande in 1846 to fight the Mexicans, and Texas Rangers joined the company but did not conform to U.S. Army discipline or adopt a typical soldier's appearance.

When Texas seceded from the Union in 1861, United States troops withdrew from the state, leaving the frontier unprotected. Corrupt politicians caused the Rangers to be disbanded, and the frontier became unsafe, with terrible outlawry by Mexican bandits who rode across the Rio

Grande to steal Texas cattle. In 1874 the Rangers reorganized into a single company called the Frontier Battalion.

The Texas Rangers had a reputation for harassing Indians and Mexicans who lived near the border. Rangers of the late nineteenth and early twentieth centuries tortured and murdered many Mexicans, making it necessary for the state legislature to curtail the Rangers' authority. Waco's Texas Ranger Hall of Fame, built in 1968, is dedicated to the history of Texas law enforcement. An array of valuable guns (including one owned by Billy the Kid), Texas Ranger artifacts, and historical paintings comprise the core of the museum's collection. Also at the complex is Fort Fisher, an architecturally accurate reconstruction of the fieldstone outpost built in 1837 for the Texas Rangers; it is now home for Ranger Company F.

There is a small admission charge for the Texas Ranger Hall of Fame. Hours are 9:00 A.M. to 5:00 P.M. daily (till 6:00 P.M. June through August).

The Real Ima Hogg

Ima Hogg was the only daughter of James Stephen Hogg, first native Texas governor, who served from 1890 to 1895. Hogg was one of the most popular governors in Texas history; among his greatest accomplishments were organizing the state railroad commission and founding Texaco.

Ima was a wealthy Houston philanthropist until her death in 1975, at age ninety-three. She was named after the heroine of a long epic poem written by her uncle. Rumors of sisters named "Ura" and "Wera" are false; Ima had two younger brothers. Ima's name has long been the source of jokes, but she gained the respect of the community for her devotion to fund-raising for charities and supporting the arts. She also donated a large parcel of land to the University of Texas, and restored her father's first plantation and made it a state park.

Her home, Bayou Bend, is in Houston. The Hogg family built the pink stucco house in 1926 and incorporated cast-iron architectural details reminiscent of New Orleans and the Gulf Coast. Originally the house was built to be the residence for Ima and her two brothers, but Mike Hogg moved out when he married in 1929 and Will Hogg died in 1930.

Ima began collecting art and antiques, which she planned to donate one day to the City of Houston. After World War I, she purchased old china and glass to furnish Bayou Bend and developed a keen interest in early colonial furniture. Some of her major acquisitions that have been put on public display at Bayou Bend include a lady's desk made by Boston cabinetmakers, a rare Massachusetts chair-back settee with eight matching chairs, and numerous pieces of Tucker porcelain from Philadelphia. The paintings she collected, most by major eighteenth- and nineteenth-century artists including Gilbert Stuart, Charles Wilson Peale, and John Singleton Copley, are on display at Bayou Bend, as are a collection of American silver pieces crafted by Paul Revere and pre–Revolutionary War porcelain made by the Bonnin and Morris company.

In her late seventies, Ima began the complex process of converting her home into a museum. In 1965 she moved from Bayou Bend to a high-rise apartment nearby. The remarkable nineteen-room Bayou Bend collection, which was formally dedicated and opened to the public in March 1966, comprises more than 4,000 objects that range from the mid–seventeenth century to the third quarter of the nineteenth century.

Bayou Bend and its beautiful gardens are open to the public. Guests are escorted in groups of four by well-versed docents; tours last approximately an hour and a half. (Visitors are requested to wear soft-soled shoes to protect the floors.) Hours are 10:00 A.M. to 2:30 P.M. Tuesday through Friday; 10:00 A.M. to 1:30 P.M. Saturday; and 1:00 to 5:00 P.M. on the second Sunday of each month (except March). Bayou Bend is closed in August. Make reservations by calling (713) 529-8773.

The Palace on Wheels

The Atalanta is the private railroad car that belonged to Jay Gould, the railroad tycoon who was the richest man in the United States. Gould had his private car built in 1888 by American Car & Foundry. Made of solid wood, with an observation platform entirely of brass, the Atalanta is true to the flamboyant Gay Nineties. The eighty-eight-foot-long palace on wheels has four staterooms, lounge, dining room, kitchen, butler's pantry, and bathroom with a silver wash-bowl. Two maple-paneled staterooms boast beautiful book-cases, china cabinets, and several portraits of members of the Gould family. The wood paneling in the guest room is covered with satin imported from India. In the master bed-room Gould's son George had a secret compartment built in the wall for hiding jewelry and money.

Jay Gould never traveled without the comforts of a mil-lionaire: he took along his private physician and a special chef, and often a cow was kept in the baggage car to provide fresh milk and butter. Formal dress was always required in the dining car, where the silverware, from Tiffany's, was engraved "Car Atalanta." Even the butler's pantry and the kitchen were furnished with the best of everything, includ-ing glass decorations on the iceboxes, a rare luxury in the nineteenth century. The kitchen floor is lined with copper and all the original water piping is of solid brass. Pearl buzzers in every room were used to call the porter for assis-tance.

Jay Gould's private railroad car . . . a palace on wheels!
(Photo by Ken Everett. Courtesy Jessie Allen Wise Garden Club)

During a severe housing shortage in the 1930s, Gould's car was taken to East Texas by the Texas & Pacific Railroad company and used by its yardmaster, Mr. J. T. Davis, and his family, for temporary living quarters. The Davis family liked it so much they stayed for thirteen years. The car was later sold to the Jessie Allen Wise Garden Club of Jefferson, Texas, and is now a public museum. It is open daily for tours. For reservations and more information, call (214) 665-2513.

Think Pink

When you hear the name Mary Kay, there is a tendency automatically to *think pink*, and for good reason. The highly successful Dallas-based cosmetics firm has used the color pink to promote its products since the company was founded by Mary Kay Ash in 1963.

Mary Kay states that she originally wanted to use a feminine color to package her merchandise, and that "delicate pink seemed to look prettier than anything else in white tile bathrooms." She carried the pink theme even further when the company began awarding pink Cadillacs to its top salespeople. In fact, the firm places such a large car order each year that General Motors has named the color "Mary Kay Pink." It is spectacular to visit Dallas during a Mary Kay sales seminar and see an enormous parking lot next to the Dallas Convention Center filled with a sea of pink automobiles!

While pink Cadillacs are identified with Mary Kay Cosmetics, they aren't the company's only pink vehicles. There is also a fleet of pink trailer trucks. When these babies speed down the interstate, it commands about as much attention as a pink elephant!

A fleet of pink Cadillacs and Mary Kay representatives in front of the Dallas headquarters. (Courtesy Mary Kay Cosmetics, Inc.)

Santa Claus: The Bank Robber

Probably the most famous bank robbery in Texas history was committed by Santa Claus, who robbed the First National Bank in Cisco on December 23, 1927. While the small western Texas town was celebrating Yuletide spirit, a man dressed as Santa Claus and three accomplices held up the local bank, stealing $12,200 in cash and $150,000 in securities. The Santa Claus bandit, Marshall Ratliff, then escaped with his accomplices, holding two little girls as hostages.

Chief of Police G. E. Bedford raced to the scene and waited in the alley behind the bank, while other officers took stations nearby. After exiting the bank, the bandits stole a sedan and sped down the alley; they shot Chief Bedford to death with five bullets and wounded two other policemen. One of the robbers, Louis Davis, was wounded during the escape. When the sedan eventually ran out of gas, the bandits stopped a car and forced the occupants out. They transferred the loot and the wounded Davis to the second car but soon realized they did not have a key. The police were approaching, so the three robbers decided to leave Davis behind and return to the original car. They sped off once more, only to discover they had left the money behind!

A chase followed. The bandits had risked their lives and now had a flat tire, no money, and no gas. They pulled over to the side of the road, left the two girls behind, and ran into the brush. Santa Claus, who was injured, limped away into the woods.

Over 100 men joined in a posse. Sheriffs and deputies from eight different counties and many outraged citizens volunteered their services. The search went on until December 27, when the three fugitives were finally caught. Ratliff had six bullet wounds and Henry Helms had been shot seven times, while twenty-two-year-old Robert Hill escaped injury.

The three men were tried, and the jury sentenced Ratliff and Helms to death. Hill was jailed and was later released on good behavior. He is currently a model citizen and lives under an assumed name in West Texas. Helms was executed on September 6, 1929. Ratliff remained on death row.

On November 18, 1929, Ratliff escaped, supplied with a .38 Colt pistol he had found in a jailer's desk drawer. He killed a policeman affectionately known in the Cisco community as Uncle Tom. Ratliff was captured and taken back to jail. The next day an angry mob forced its way into the jail, took Ratliff a block away, and lynched him.

Six people were killed and eight injured in the Santa Claus caper.

The Rangerettes of Kilgore

The Rangerettes were the first precision dance-drill team to bring high-kicking show biz to the football field; their reputation stretches far beyond the Texas border. The Kilgore College Rangerette Drill Team, perhaps the most sought-after collegiate performing group in the world, has toured all over the globe—the Far East, South America, Europe, and behind the Iron Curtain, in Romania. They have made countless appearances on television shows, including *The Ed Sullivan Show;* have been the subject of a *60 Minutes* report; and have been photographed for the pages of *Sports Illustrated, Newsweek,* and *Life.*

Gussie Nell Davis organized the country's first college drill team in 1940. Now the sixty-five-member drill squad is as American as apple pie, and football halftimes are incomplete without their performances. This unique form of American culture landed the Rangerettes a permanent display in the Contemporary Arts Museum in Houston, which has pronounced them a "living art form."

Five officers in white and forty-eight Rangerettes in traditional red, white, and blue Texas-style uniforms (the design is copyrighted) are usually accompanied by the Kilgore College Ranger Band.

A Deliberate Disaster

In the summer of 1896, general agent William G. Crush (aptly, but coincidentally, named) of the Katy Railroad passenger service staged a deliberate collision to drum up business. To his mind, the railroad needed a spectacular public relations event, and believe it or not, he concocted a bona fide calamity to fill the bill. Crush arranged for two powerful 1865 vintage locomotives to crash head-on at full speed—a perfect opportunity to draw interest from all corners of the U.S.

A site just north of Waco was selected for the disaster, and the dueling ground was to be a five-mile section of track, long enough to permit the two engines to build deadly momentum. Promotion announcements and invitations were distributed across the country, the media picked up the story, and enough attention was generated to require a grandstand to accommodate the crowd of 30,000 spectators gathered to witness the event. Two hundred guards were employed to keep people in safe areas.

In true western fashion, at high noon on September 15, 1896, the two mighty engines lurched toward each other. The crowd went wild as the trains cruised to a speed of sixty miles an hour. With throttle wide open, each crewman jumped from his respective train to safety. From a distance they watched their abandoned vessels collide.

Those who came to see a spectacular smashup got their

The crowd at the wreck.
(All photos courtesy The Texas Collection, Baylor University, Waco)

Full steam ahead!

money's worth—the crash lit up the prairie for miles in all directions. Unplanned, however, was the boiler explosion in both engines, which caused steam-heated shrapnel to bombard the panic-stricken spectators, killing two and injuring

The trains collide.

The explosion.

more than fifty. Fortunately for the railroad, the incident occurred before the days of class-action suits; Katy officials were able to settle out of court for peanuts. Predictably, authorities blamed the crash on Crush.

The Traveling Hotel

The Fairmount Hotel of San Antonio won a place in the *Guinness Book of World Records* as the largest building ever to be moved. In 1985 the three-story, 16,500-square-foot brick building was relocated from one site to another in the La Villita historical district. Moving the hotel, which weighed in at 3.2 million pounds, took thirty-six dollies with pneumatic tires and was completed in six days.

The Fairmount, which opened its doors in 1906, originally operated as a residential hotel, but by the 1980s it had become shabby. When it was decided that the hotel would be razed and a shopping mall built on the site, the San Antonio Conservation Society stepped in. A location six blocks down the street and across a bridge was found, and the hotel was moved. A $4-million-dollar renovation project renewed the hotel's original splendor: the U-shaped Fairmount was carefully restored to its original Italianate Victorian style by three Texans who then established the Fairmount Hotel Company. The interior is classically furnished; each room has expansive windows, eighteen-foot-high ceilings, and a marble bathroom. The hotel is about three blocks south of the Alamo. For reservations, call (800) 642-3363, or in Texas (512) 224-8800.

Funeral for a Baby-blue Ferrari

Before her death in 1977, Sandra Ilene West requested to be buried in her baby-blue 1964 Ferrari. Wearing her favorite lace nightgown, she was placed in the reclined driver's seat. In her will she specified that the automobile be placed in a large coffin/box before being lowered into the grave. The tomb was filled with two truckloads of cement to discourage vandals.

The Dallas skyline.
(Courtesy Dallas Convention & Visitors Bureau)